22 WAYS TO TACKLE SUCCESS

Steps to Becoming a Better You!

DEJUAN GOSSETT

22 Ways to Tackle Success – Steps to Becoming a Better You
by DeJuan Gossett

Inspired Press Publisher
1333 Chelsea Court
Morrow, OH 45152

www.inspiredpresspublisher.com
513-256-1792

ISBN: 978-1-7336423-0-9

Library of Congress Control Number: 2019900835

TABLE OF CONTENTS

NOTE FROM THE AUTHOR

My children Maria, Dylan, Max, and Keegan. Always give your best, be respectful, and never give up on your dreams. The world is yours.

To my family, for the support that they have provided through my ups and my downs.

Special thanks to my friends who helped put a dent in this book, and a rock star in particular that truly pushed this over the top. Your honesty, critiques and advice have been critical in refining the creative process.

To my Power Team: Athletic trainer, the late Bill Walker; my surgeon, Dr. Angilo Colosimo; rehab coordinator, Pat Graman; and my strength coach, Micky Marotti. Thank you for your continued optimism and dedication of defying the odds throughout my recovery and patching me back both physically and mentally.

To Donna, and her team at Inspired Press Publisher. Thank you for your patience and the hours you spent working with me. I am forever grateful.

To every individual I have had the opportunity to lead or be led by, I want to say thank you for being the inspiration and foundation for 22 Ways to Tackle Success. This experience has been internally challenging and extremely rewarding.

Learn more about what I am involved with at my website and social media accounts. I would love to hear your feedback, answer questions or for you to leave a review.

www.22WTTS.com
www.twitter.com/22_WTTS
www.instagram.com/22_WTTS
www.facebook.com/22waystotacklesuccess

INTRODUCTION

I have always focused on the road to success. It has been woven within the fabric of my soul since I was a boy. I would walk up and down Mayfair Drive looking for someone to challenge in any and everything. Sports were the dominant choice, as our little street was filled with adolescent boys of different ages. I wanted to be the alpha dog, but that spot was occupied by Shawn Turner. Shawn was in high school, and the closest description I can give would be the New York Yankees 6'6" home run slugger, Aaron Judge. This guy had an arm of Roger Clemens and a Dennis Rodman attitude. When I saw Shawn with his swag and bravado, as he walked up the hill to pitch another no hitter in his baseball game, I set a goal that I would be that guy one day. I wasn't the biggest kid growing up, as I wrestled in the 95-pound division in eighth grade, but I would fight you tooth-and-nail. When I wrote this book, I found a picture of when I came in second place in a tournament. You would have thought the world had ended. I now look back and realize that I am happy I carry the burning desire to be my best in everything that I do just as I did that day in the eighth grade.

Success didn't seem like an illusion to me at any time because I had it engraved in my mind that my story would be one that would inspire others. I have been blessed to attain success as a college football player and as a professional in the business world throughout my life. I soared on the wings of being a rising star as a 17-year-old freshman until a tragic injury occurred and changed the course of my journey. They called me "The Medical Miracle" because nobody had come back from an injury this gruesome before. Not only did I come back from it, but I went on to be a four-year starter, the #2 solo tackler in school history, and top 10 in total tackles at The University of Cincinnati. This success led me to reach my ultimate goal: the NFL! I experienced the greatest day in my life when I signed with the New York Giants in 2002, only to experience disappointment once again, as I was forced to retire less than a year later when it was discovered that I had torn the same ACL in preparation for training camp.

The experience was challenging yet enlightening. It brought a lot of pain embedded in lessons that life had to teach to me, which prepared me for my post-football career. After recovering from my injuries, I had many successes in the business world, as we made a mini fortune in real estate before the 2007 market crash came down on us like Samson and brought us to our knees. I fought and came back, and today, I am doing what I love; helping others. I'm an employee benefits consultant, which means that I help companies mitigate risk and reduce costs on their insurance expenditures. I thought the legendary Pro Bowl running back Edgerrin James was a tough one to tackle until I ran up on the ever-changing healthcare market. I didn't get in the record books for nothing, as my clients and I utilize a lot of these steps in the book to tackle healthcare just like we do success. After thought and prayer and overcoming my own fears of writing, I decided to share my experience through this book to inspire and nurture others through my pain, failures and triumphs.

You might be thinking that life is a challenge and wondering if success will ever be within your grasp. I know that overwhelming feeling when you feel defeated and going nowhere fast, but I also know that you can come out of that phase in life if you are rightly guided. I discovered these steps through my own challenging experiences, and I am optimistic that if you follow through with the tips shared in this book, you will be triumphant in your mission, and your success story will be your blessing to others for years to come.

My dream for this book is not just to inspire you individually, but to bring more attention to helping less-privileged children who don't have the opportunity to start on the level ground. I want them to see the importance of gaining an education and learning what it takes to succeed in the face of adversity. Everyone can win in life. It is possible to be the very best at what you do and make a difference in the lives of others. I want to share my battles and offer tried and tested ways that have worked for me and others. This book is my way of giving back to society and reaching out to those who are constantly growing in their personal journeys, as well as those who haven't yet found their footing.

Be rest assured that everything you find in this book is practical and workable if you put your mind to it. We will begin our journey with a key word: passion. You will glean more about passion as we go on, but as you read on, I urge you to be passionate enough to take decisive steps about what you learn, and some things may be reinforcement to things that you already know.

Do not read to forget. Get a journal by your side as we go through this voyage and take notes, so that we can prepare or enhance your action plans. Decide on what you will do with every step shared here. Don't hold back. You will be amazed at the level of success you experience. I am incredibly excited and humbled to be sharing my thoughts and experiences with you. I thank you for coming on this journey with me. Enough talk! Let's get right to it and tackle success from the ground up. START NOW!

CHAPTER ONE

PASSION

When I think about my days with The University of Cincinnati football team, I remember the one thing that saw me through all of the two-a-day practices in the blistering summer sun, the 5 a.m. morning runs in Nippert Stadium before a day full of classes, and the constant bumps and bruises that had us popping ibuprofen like they were the newest flavour of skittles. Passion. What better way to begin this book? Passion is that high, intense, powerful emotion that cements your belief in a thing or activity without wavering. Anytime you find yourself wondering what distinguishes you from that man or woman who is tagged "successful," remember this word: passion. It will take you places money and influence won't. It will help you soar on the wings of success and never falter because, regardless of where you find yourself, with passion you can do BIG THINGS.

A passionate individual is one who is consumed with the idea of winning. Some would call it fanatical, but best believe that person wins at every turn because passion is also a mindset that sets you apart from others. I had a coach in college named Rick Smith who always said, "You either get better or you get worse. You only stay the same when you are dead." I didn't ask questions because he was quick to hand out gassers (an insane running drill), but boy he had some passion behind what he said, no matter what it was. His point was to eliminate complacency and always strive to be better every day. Sticks with me today because I'm not ready to turn out the lights, and I'm not going backward. If we are passionate about getting better in some capacity every day, we will have little victories day after day that will lead to our bigger accomplishments down the road.

As a youth, I grew up as an elite baseball player, but I always dreamed of being a football star. There were no girls in the stands at the baseball game and as good as I was, I didn't have passion to get better daily on the baseball field. I was passionate about not liking to strike out and I displayed that with my dugout tantrums that drew the ire of my watchful mother, but that was more a reflection of my passion to be successful. Due to my diminutive stature which I spoke about in the Introduction, football wasn't in the cards until later in my high school years at Wyoming High School. In my freshman year, I did not play football as I convinced myself that I was too small, and my life would be in danger out there with those goliaths. I started my career during an unsanctioned football game in the open field parallel to the stadium, as the Cowboys were playing under the lights. A group of us decided it was a great idea to play tackle football without pads and that was a recipe for fireworks. We were five minutes in, and these kids from another neighbourhood arrived. You could tell they were outsiders and honestly, they were intimidating. They were dominating my friends, and I decided that I had enough. The biggest kid had the ball running through an open hole because none of my guys dared to challenge him. I channelled my inner Ronnie Lott, possibly the hardest hitting safety to ever play football, and zeroed in on my target: I wrapped him up at the waist, brought my hips, lifted him off the ground as I drove him backward and planted him on the grass to a loud thud. You could feel the tension as all went quiet, and this time my passion for helping others and winning just got me into a fist fight with a big bad wolf from a neighbourhood that my friends and I typically would not challenge. I don't condone fighting among youths, so I won't go into details, but let's just say the Wyoming football team wasn't the only one that won that night. A legend was born in a dirt field, and my passion for football had risen.

In my sophomore year of high school, I joined the football team, and it was the greatest decision of my young life. My first year on the team, I didn't start immediately at the varsity level, but I did earn a spot as the "missile" on the kick-off team. With this role, you have no responsibility other than to tackle the ball carrier. This was perfect in my eyes, and I was ecstatic that my efforts in training camp earned me a position with the big boys. My first game was a humid Friday night. I looked so clean in my uniform, you would have thought Deion Sanders had joined the Cowboys high school team. We were the first to kick-off, and I was so nervous I could feel my legs shaking as the referee blew the whistle for our kicker to kick-off. He dropped his hand and I shot out like a rocket. It's amazing how fast you can run when you use fear as fuel. I zipped in and out of blockers and just like the previous year in my unsanctioned football game, I lit the ball carrier up to *oohs* and cheers from the crowd.

I became hooked on the feeling of accomplishment this gave me, and I grew passionate about getting it repeatedly. I played with great players and coaches at Wyoming and eventually earned a football scholarship to the University of Cincinnati. I was recruited by the current Baltimore Ravens Head Coach, John Harbaugh. By this time, I had developed my skills and knowledge of the game, so it was an excellent opportunity to showcase my youthful dreams. I wanted to be the best to ever play the game. Ambition got me there, but I didn't foresee the troubles ahead.

I remember the first time I saw my name in a magazine. It was the summer after my senior year in high school, and a popular national publication had its college preview magazine on the shelves. I wanted to look at the depth chart because I am fanatical about planning and executing my pursuit to the top. I see a section under the Bearcats labelled future star and there it was:

**DEJUAN GOSSETT ... hidden gem
of the Bearcats recruiting class and the type
of local recruit the Bearcats need to take the
program to another level.**

I used my graduation money to buy the magazine because (I haven't mentioned this yet) I grew up on a single-mom's teacher salary with three kids, and so extra money for a magazine was a big deal to me. I shared this article with everyone I saw for the next two weeks and slept with it under my pillow in the bunkbed that I shared with my baby brother until I worried that I would wrinkle the cover in my sleep. I was living my dream.

I arrive on campus, and things couldn't have gone any better. I showed that I belonged as I skyrocketed up the depth chart in Rex Ryan's sixteenth-ranked national defense. Two days before our season opener, and I was set to start in the secondary as a true freshman surrounded by three future NFL studs (Sam Garnes, Chris Hewitt, Artrell Hawkins). I was on the top of the world with my head high and chest puffed like a rugged veteran—until the music stopped, and it all came crashing to a halt. I tore my ACL, LLC, PCL, and both meniscus 15 minutes into that final preparation practice. My knee literally went backward and to the side 90 degrees. Dr. Colosimo described my injury as the worse he had ever seen, and they weren't sure that I would ever be able to play football again—in fact, they were hoping that I would be able to walk without a limp for the rest of my life at best. Less than 30 days on campus, and my dream had turned into a tragic nightmare. Players describe the screams of pain that came from my lungs as one of the most heart-breaking moments of their lives.

It was honestly the worst phase of my own life, even now as I look back as a seasoned 40-year-old. I kept asking internally, "why me?" Why should this happen to me at the start of my career as I tried to grapple with these emotions as a 17-year-old kid. I still remember asking Dr. Colosimo after they carried me off the field "can I play this Saturday," as I hid my tears and sat in pain as my entire leg felt as if it were on fire. I couldn't get the pain to stop, and I cried myself to sleep at night. How did I spend my eighteenth birthday? Hours of reconstructive surgery and a party full of nurses and doctors, as my brothers played on without me. I felt alone, confused and unfulfilled.

Dr. Colosimo and his team did a great job on the surgery. The late Bill Walker and his team set the recovery plan with Mickey Marrotti and Pat Graman said, "I believe in you. Let's defy odds and get you on the field again." I pulled up my boot straps and grabbed the opportunity with both hands because their optimism was the spark I needed to come out of the funk. We will talk about this later, but to do the impossible, you will need a plan and a power team. However, it was ultimately my passion for the game that helped me to make that decision to put the doubt at bay and say #22 is coming back to play. That was a good one, right? I digress.

You see, the most striking thing about passion is that if you hold on and keep that fire lit, it will never go away. I had a series of experiences just after this initial injury which I will share with you later, but just know that I made it. The great thing is that you can too, no matter the odds or diagnosis. Life will always throw stuff at you. You will get to your lowest ebb and wonder if you're going to make it. You will question your decisions and think about them repeatedly, but through it all, if you are a man or a woman of passion, you will have a success story to share at the end.

It doesn't matter where you are now, or where you have been in the past. Ignite the passion from within you. Cast your mind back to what propelled you forward to pursue your dream and allow yourself to relive that idea. It is the starting point to building passion. After doing this, don't let go! So many people have given up on their dream and regretted it later in life. Don't be a statistic due to circumstance or fear. Whenever you have challenges along your path, your dream will always keep you focused. It is passion that will see you through, because at times tackling success involves pushing yourself beyond your own comfort and proving to yourself just how special you are.

I sit with you today with the ability to put down my thoughts because despite the lemons given to me throughout my life, and believe me there were many, I was able to make lemonade. The passion I have for success made it possible for me to press on, so I can inspire and uplift someone else. The great thing is I am still in the fight because I'm just like you—unless you are Bill Gates or Jay-Z. The funny thing is that they are still in the fight too, because as successful as they are to their standards, they have a passion to be better and do better. They will always be tackling new goals and dreams, just on a different level. You can be the best version of who you are right now if you are passionate and committed to your own individual dream. It is your dream and aspiration as such. No one will keep the fire burning for you, so find what makes you click—and "Let's Go!" We have embarked on this journey to success together, and passion has been a great start. Are you feeling inspired already? Fantastic! It's going to get better, so stick with me as we tackle the next step.

CHAPTER TWO

CREATE A PLAN

Whether you are selling insurance or playing soccer, creating a start-up or leading an organization, passion is vital to achieve and sustain success. However, it doesn't stop at being passionate. You need a plan. A plan will provide the roadmap to close the gap between where you are today and where you would like to be. The road to success is like building a house. When you want to build a home, you start out with an idea or a vision. This plan details everything about the building process—from the foundation to the structure, windows, doors, etc. Once you have a plan and you round up your support, the building can commence. As you go on, there will be times when you need to go back to the drawing board and check for the next step to continue to move forward along your path. When it comes to achieving success, utilizing your plan is crucial.

When I work with clients, I always want to know what success looks like for them as a company and sometimes individually. Armed with this information, I can tailor a plan that covers every aspect of this business, and we will follow a detailed roadmap to achieve the ultimate success. This process is something that we come back to often because utilizing a plan for success is not a set-it-and-forget-it process. It's a guide, and typically your ability to succeed will only be as good as your commitment to the execution of your plan. This is saying that if you start your journey with the right map, you will have amazing success stories to go with it.

Alright, let's say that you are a young student who wants to improve your performance and make the dean's list. This is what success means to you. You need to devise a plan that includes your study sessions, visits to the library, a strict schedule that entails completing assignments on time, and being a problem-solver as you make your mark in the classroom. Some would consider this process similar to time management, which makes sense because most individuals that excel with time management follow a strict plan. Consider time management as a complement to your plan and a skill that will provide you with a better foundation to execute your plan. So, whenever you feel lost throughout the journey, you can always go back to your plan and be reminded of what needs to be done.

I had a plan as a football player, just as I have a plan now as a consultant for my clients. My plan covered every aspect of my football career and I was continually going back to it for next steps and checking off my small wins along the way. After my surgeries, my plan was to shock the world and get back in uniform with my brothers and play football again. When I reached that goal in six months, with what was expected to last as long as a year away from the field, I set my sights on a starting position on defense. Once I won the job coming out of spring practice to the amazement of everyone, my plan was to make it to the NFL. Amazingly, I was able to do that as well.

It might sound redundant, but if you want something, create a plan and grind until you reach your goals. Don't let anything stand in your way. Follow the roadmap you created. My doctors and trainers devised a plan that would give me the best chance to return to football after the injury. It involved strict exercise routines and therapy sessions that aided relief and improved my strength after I had lost 60 pounds and muscle to atrophy. I went from having the arms of Popeye to skinny legs like Olive Oyl. I honestly looked sick and helpless, and mentally I was succumbing to that narrative. The doctors needed to dig deep to bring me back to life. The program also gave me hope for the future. Even though many doubted if I would ever play again, I always knew I would make a comeback because every time I looked at my plan, I regained confidence and held on to that dream. It's such a common statement but resonates to this day: Failing to prepare is preparing to fail. Don't tell me you want to get somewhere if you haven't thought about what it's going to take. That's called a wish and unless you have a Genie, it's unlikely to come to fruition.

A plan will help you put things into perspective as you get to know exactly how real your thoughts on success are and the possibility of bringing these ideas to life. A lot of people struggle with success because they have failed in connecting their dreams with reality. They have a whole lot of thoughts, but these thought patterns aren't in sync with their reality; they experience overwhelming issues that contribute to them giving up entirely.

Here is the critical point: Your plan should be realistic. It should be filled with plausible ideas on how you can reach your expected end, and it should be a plan you can bank on any day and any time. When you sit down to work out the plan consider every aspect of your dream, every detail, concept and activity. If you capture the whole of it, nothing will take you by surprise. You will have challenges yes, but those problems will be surmountable for you because you've got a plan.

Your plan is the doorway to success. You shouldn't get lost, and you will always know what to do because you've armed yourself with a plan and passionate mind-set; in the end, the world will be yours. Nothing can stop a person who is determined to succeed, but above all, nothing can stop a person who is armed with a plan to make it happen. We will be making another stop on our journey, and you will love the message embedded in that section.

Guess what? We are going BIG!

CHAPTER THREE

THINK BIG, DREAM BIGGER

I mentioned thinking big and dreaming bigger in the previous chapter, and the importance cannot be overemphasized when talking about success. I wanted to be the best football player in the world and showcase my talents in front of millions in the stadiums and on TV. I wanted a big car, a big house, and to be able to leave a legacy while setting my family up financially for generations to come. My hope was that we would never have to struggle again like we did as I was growing up. No more evictions, repossessions or food stamps. Most leaders and innovators have unrealistic expectations and visions. This is what makes them special. I had a huge dream backed by a plan and a passionate mind-set. Dreaming big makes it possible for you to reach for the stars. It gives you the motivation to knock out that extra rep, write that extra research assignment, or perfect your craft. When you are dreaming big and willing to put work behind it, anything is possible. I tell young people to dream often. Don't restrict your ability to imagine. Don't think it's too big and impossible. Don't assume that you don't have what it takes to achieve such dreams.

People often talk themselves out of their dreams; they look around at their current state and allow what they see to affect their mindset and ability to see farther. So, you want to be a doctor? There you are visualizing it and then stop abruptly because you remembered that you live in the projects with no one to help you take the steps to get there. Take a step back. Who says you cannot make it from where you are? Don't be your voice of failure. Be free to dream, free to go bigger and free to be who you want to be.

The best form of success you can ever experience is the feeling of freedom from your own doubts. When you dream small, you open yourself up to achieving very little because you attract what you think the most. You ultimately become what you believe about yourself. Wake up every morning with thoughts of possibility, see beyond the world around you and trust your dreams. I remember lying on that hospital bed with my mom by my side, reassuring me that all will be fine. I could see in her eyes that she had fears of her own but wanted to be strong for me. I looked around and saw the nurses trying their best to bring me comfort, I saw the bloody staples in my knee, and I was in so much pain that I was on the brink of losing consciousness. I shut my eyes for a few seconds and went back to who I believed I was meant to be; a football star. At that point in time, I didn't see the miserable situation, I saw myself on the turf of Nippert Stadium, with thousands of people watching and cheering me on. I saw my dream, and my heart was at peace.

Don't allow anyone, anything, or any situation to come between you and your dreams. The best ability you can always have at your disposal is the ability to have a short memory like a defensive back in football or an artist after a poor performance. If a defensive back relishes in the last bad play, that negativity will carry on to the next and snowball. Life is the same way, so continue to embrace your dream regardless of what you may experience. If the thought is big enough, chances are you will be able to accomplish whatever it is. If you don't get to the stars, you will surely catch a glimpse of the skies. Big dreams aren't meant for "big" people. They are for everyone who dares to take the bold **BIG STEP**. If you have been creating dreams based on your current environment or based on what others feel you can accomplish, it's time to make a U-turn and start dreaming for you. Look within and ask yourself what you want. I always ask myself this question, "What will I do if I weren't afraid?" Come on. Ask yourself that question often. What would you do if you didn't have any restrictions or thoughts of impossibility?

You must dream, and it must be big—bigger than life, bigger than anything you ever thought you could do. It doesn't stop at dreaming. You must know in your heart that it is possible for you to achieve the dreams. Former New York mayor Mark Bloomberg once said, "Telling me something is impossible is like waving a red flag in front of a bull." I love that statement because if we truly want something and go about it the appropriate way, nothing can stop us. Go Big or Go Home!

We are gradually taking things up a notch as we ramp up our preparation. Hopefully, every section is getting better and better for you as you prepare to put this book down after Chapter 22 and get started on your path. Which is why the next segment is going to be all about you. Yes, you. Get ready to fall in love and find yourself.

CHAPTER FOUR

FIND YOURSELF, LOVE WHAT YOU DO

James Altucher once said, "The choices you make today will be your biography tomorrow." When I read that, I think one of the hardest parts we have when tackling success is losing oneself on the journey. I've seen and experienced where there is such a focus on winning that we forget to enjoy ourselves. I have all this money, but I hate my career. It effects my family and my health. I'm a great ballplayer, but I only play because I know my parents love it. That's the only time they show me attention. I would rather be in the band with my friends. These types of things occur every day. The times when we genuinely find ourselves, define the measure of success we attain and the story that we leave for others to tell when our expiration date comes. How do you want your story to be told?

John Doe worked tirelessly at a dead-end job living paycheck to paycheck, but he always dreamed of owning his own business until his last days. That made me sad just writing it. I think about so many individuals in this world not doing what truly makes them happy on a daily basis. There is a secure connection between finding yourself and loving what you do. When I started out my professional career in sales, it was because of the love I had for competition and money, but I lost myself in the process. Even though I was winning, I couldn't function at my very best. It wasn't until I realized that my happiness comes from helping others rather than selling products or services. My numbers only sky rocketed because my pursuit for greatness is pure. My "passion" is in helping and creating solutions, so it fueled my growth and satisfaction.

Oprah Winfrey recently said, "The key to fulfilment, success, happiness and contentment in life, is when you align your personality with what your soul actually came to do." I completely agree.

The process of finding yourself is always deep. You have to stay in touch with who you are every day while keeping your eyes on the prize. Getting close to your dreams gives you a feeling of inertia that can make you lose touch with who you are, to where you can become an entirely new person and miss your way. This is often the case with superstars. They attain a level of success but can no longer recognize the person that they have become.

Find yourself as you embark on your journey to success. As you look in the mirror every day, be reminded of who you are and what you stand for. A person who never loses touch with who he or she is, will always keep an eye fixed on the prize and never back down when a challenge rears its ugly head. I got to understand this principle of success at my lowest point in life, and since then I haven't lost touch with who I am. I know what I want and what I have to do to get it. This is what it means to find yourself and be who you are while loving what you do.

Loving what you do is not negotiable if you want to succeed, so you can't escape it. I loved being a football player. It was a part of me, and still is today. Football gave me something to look forward to every day, but now I simply turn my career into the same challenges that I faced on the gridiron. I love working with my clients as we strategize in the offseason like Bill Belichick and the Patriots and execute like champions when it comes time for renewals. Work and career become easy when you love what you do. Loving what you do makes you innovative, creative and passionate. It makes you put in extra hours when everyone else is kicking back. It helps you get the most out of what you do and keeps you ahead of the game. Game-changers love what they do. They feel a sense of joy and pride being involved with their career and this translates into success for them.

When you simply tolerate your job, business, career or task at hand, it becomes burdensome for you. There is a sense of laziness attached to people who don't love what they do. They go about their business watching the clock and waiting for the day to be over. If you want success with fulfilment, then you have to love what you do. Fall in love with your dream so much that it is all you think about. You will always do well with something that is manifested from your heart. The first step is to find yourself. Don't lose sight of who you are and remain focused on what you seek to attain. The second level is to fall in love with what you do, your business, your career or job. Allow joy to radiate from within you as you carry out tasks and you will experience the joys of success like never before.

We started out this chapter with a shift in focus from your work or business to you, because you are the most critical aspect of the circle of success. The importance of finding yourself while loving what you do was discussed, and we need to appreciate the connection between two concepts. The next stop is all about the power that lies within appreciation. This is my favorite aspect in life. I am so appreciative of my family, my friends, my co-workers and my clients. Because of them, I am able to wake up and do what I love every single day.

CHAPTER FIVE

BE APPRECIATIVE

Appreciation is probably the most overlooked aspect of success that most individuals haven't yet harnessed. When you are blessed to receive so much, then it is essential that you show how appreciative you are, as it opens the door for more blessings. One of the hardest things to do is to continue to be appreciative when we feel like the world is caving in on us. I want to take you back to the time I sustained my knee injuries and when I thought it was over for me. Thoughts of defeat and hopelessness serenaded my mind and I was at a loss for what to do. It felt like I wasn't going to come out of the hospital alive and well again, so I almost drowned in a sea of fear and anxiety.

Gratitude got me out of that fragile mental state. When my mom came into the hospital room and wiped away the tears, she also spoke to me about the importance of staying grateful in the midst of the challenges and problems. I was amazed at her level of optimism as she watched her oldest son, "Superman," down and out under a single white linen hospital sheet. So here I am, big football player, lying down and thinking the world is over for me. I take a look at my mom, and I started to count my blessings. She sacrificed so much so that I could play this game at a high level. I thought about the days that we lived in the oldest house (which used to be a post office) in Wyoming, so that I could go to a great school and not be a statistic. We were bare bones poor during this time, but we had each other. I had my younger siblings watching to see how their older brother would react to this situation.

My brother Christopher had been a fan favorite ever since he ran onto the basketball court during a game my freshman year in high school. Apparently, I looked parched as he sprinted across the floor yelling my name holding out the cup of Sprite that he had just gotten from the concession stand. I had to stand up and show him I would not quit in the face of adversity. I looked at my future, the coaches, and the fact that I had a life, which means I had hope and began to appreciate all that I had. From the moment I practiced being appreciative for things that I simply took for granted, things began to change in my approach to happiness, and I haven't stopped this attitude since that day.

I will say that I am human, and I have faltered along the way. There have been many times where I felt like dropping to my knees to ask, "why me?" But, when I re-center my perspective around gratitude, I always win the battle. Granny would tell us to count our blessings and not our worries. That is so true, as a positive thought can change your whole outlook on life.

Sometimes in life, we look at the glimpse of success we attain and get lost in the troubles we face; unknown to us, our success lies in those times. If only we can take a break and be thankful for what we have, while looking forward to wanting to desire, we will be just fine. Success is a process. You start out with one step, and then you take several steps that lead up to a defining moment. Throughout this process, it is essential that you remain grateful.

Appreciate the times when you didn't know what to do next. Be grateful for the moments that seemed like you were stuck in one place for a very long time, and it felt like everything was crashing in on you. More importantly, be grateful for your journey. The universe has indeed blessed you, so why not give thanks. Aside from the universe, there are people in your world who have made it possible for you to dream. In my situation, I am thankful for my family, teammates, coaches, and everyone who made my recovery process possible. You see, without these people, I wouldn't have had the accomplishments that I did. It is the same with you. Look around you and identify the people who made a difference in your business, career or life in general. Show them how grateful you are through constant appreciation.

There is another side to being appreciative and it lies in the fact that when you show gratitude to someone, it triggers more of what that person had done for you. Being thankful is one of the best ways to achieve success. You will be so amazed at the level of help and assistance you get every time from the same cycle of people, just because you had shown appreciation for the ones done in the past. The next chapter looks at the role of success in guaranteeing happiness, i.e., does success bring happiness? Will you be happier when successful? Find out about this and more after you take a break and brighten someone's day with a big "I appreciate you!"

CHAPTER SIX

SUCCESS DOES NOT GUARANTEE HAPPINESS

I once heard someone say, "Happiness is in the doing, not in getting what you want." This statement triggered a thought that made me ask, "Does success guarantee happiness?" I received the answer within a short period. After asking the question, I went on a soul-searching endeavor. I looked at my life and the lives of those around me to ascertain how happy we were. We had attained a certain level of success in our minds, because success is different to everyone. I discovered that we were pleased with our level of success but weren't satisfied. We continued the grind for more, but our happiness wasn't complete.

When you get something significant done, something remarkable that leads to success, it triggers happy emotions. You feel excited and so filled with joy that you think you will always be in that state of intoxication. Sadly, you don't get to feel that way because success is an unending journey that has a lot of turns and consistent movement. Once you get over the fact that you made that singular success work, you are on the road again thinking, planning and strategizing for the next big thing. The feeling of happiness you once felt is far from you at this point, and you are back to feeling like you haven't accomplished anything.

Success does ignite the feeling of happiness, but it doesn't "guarantee" that you will be happy all the time because success is an unending journey. If you want to be truly successful, you wouldn't be satisfied with the level you've attained. You will keep pushing for more, wanting more, until you achieve it. This means that when you are met with challenges, it is hard to sustain the happiness from previous pursuits because all you're thinking about is how to win again this time around. Due to the nature of success being likened to a journey, it will be unfair to say that it is a guarantee for happiness.

The opening statement of this chapter says happiness is in the doing, meaning you find joy doing what you do. This is where your happiness lies. As you go about doing what you love and what you are passionate about, you gain satisfaction. So right now, I am genuinely pleased because writing this book is me doing what I love, what I am passionate about, reaching out to you with the message on how you can be successful in your own way. If this book turns out to be a significant success, I will be happy in that moment, but the most sustainable means of happiness already took place with me doing what I love and will continue to do for the rest of my life: sharing my life story, helping others and inspiring the next generation.

With or without the success of this book, I am happy and grateful to be doing what I love. Success becomes a bonus. Don't pin down your happiness to what you achieve, what you want or need. Just do what you love, and you will be happy. This is a vital secret to being successful in life and if you can perfect it, you can be sure that you will be completely satisfied, all the while making a difference in your life and career. If success were to guarantee happiness, then we wouldn't have the large number of "successful" people in this world dealing with anxiety and depression and turning to drugs to escape the reality that they have created, with the success that they have attained. If you take anything from this book, find joy in doing what you love and spending time with those that you love and make you truly happy.

As we move on, be reminded that you and you only are responsible for your happiness. No one will do for you what you can do for yourself. You must tell yourself that you are going to be happy regardless of the results. Success or not, you will be satisfied because you followed your path. Be serious about this. Don't let anything contradict the fact that you are going to make your life better by creating an environment conducive to being extremely happy at all times. This can be hard to do through adversity and expectations, but I know that if I can do it, you can as well. Your happiness is crucial in enhancing the next phase of this book. You will have to be thick-skinned to implement what we will be tackling next. So, put a smile on your face, laugh out loud, and tighten your sneakers, because you are about to get rid of fear and doubt.

CHAPTER SEVEN

REMOVING FEAR AND DOUBT FROM YOUR MIND

One thing that I have learned is that success cannot thrive long-term in an atmosphere of uncertainty and fear. It just doesn't work that way. If you are going to be successful, then you need to get rid of everything that pertains to doubt in your mind and thought process. Think about this for a second: Success is the accomplishment of an aim or purpose. Can you honestly say that you feel accomplished when you are afraid of any and everything? You have embarked on the most important journey of your life. It presents the perfect opportunity for you to get rid of whatever issue that doesn't suit the vision and plans you have for yourself. You are coming for what's destined to be yours and you will not be denied. Joe Vitale once said, "If you don't have some self-doubts and fears when you pursue a dream, then you haven't dreamed big enough."

DJ, you told me to get rid of them. Yes, because no doubt they are going to come as we take this ride to a place that we have never been. I would be a hypocrite if I told you that I have never encountered fear. What I want you to do is begin this journey with a clear mind and soul. Embrace your difficulties and uncertainties and execute your plan. When fear and doubt come along, we will discuss what to do with it in chapter twelve. Today, I want you to do the Connor McGregor walk of confidence as you begin on your path.

Doubt sets in when you do not think you are capable enough to do the things that guarantees success. You look at yourself with questioning eyes and hear that loud voice from within, and it continuously pulls you down. Doubt is going out the door, my friends. Doubt and unbelief in yourself will cause more harm than good to your plans. If you want to be a winner, then you must believe in yourself when nobody else does. You must look beyond your imperfections and tell yourself you can, even when it feels like you cannot. It can't be faint. It can't be just because I told you to say it. It has to come from your soul. I guarantee that if you bring passion to fuel that fire inside, it's going to be a beautiful thing when you prove to yourself and all those who ever doubted you.

I've had experiences with how demoralizing it gets with doubt. I was in a boardroom roleplaying with colleagues in front of the top-five leaders in our region. I had practiced and prepared, but my confidence wasn't there. I reached into my head for support and I was getting voicemail. This was not good, and I could not understand what was going on. These experiences affected me for the rest of the day, and it got to a point where I dreaded roleplaying. I would sit far away from my manager. I would not make eye contact. I pretended to be invisible in hopes that I wouldn't get called. Then, one morning I woke up tired of feeling that way. I wanted a change in my life. I hit the reset button and started believing in me again. My CEO at the time saw how I was being affected internally from this emotional hijacking, and we devised a plan with an executive coach. We went back to the basics and many of the steps in this book came from that experience. With an internal drive to overcome my shortcomings, along with support from my team, I saw the immense possibilities that lie within my ability to have faith in myself, and I haven't looked back since that day. The things you aren't so confident about, try them out. Come on! It is okay to fail and make mistakes. Just make sure you pick yourself up again and continue to believe in yourself. You are your superstar!

Fear creeps in as a result of doubt. It happens when you have had moments of doubts one time too many. Doubt provides the perfect breeding ground for fear to develop. Fear is a destabilizer. It destroys everything you build and brings your efforts to nothing. In the presence of fear, success can't be attained unless you can utilize it for good. Some individuals are too afraid to take the next step in life. They are so conscious of what they think will go wrong, that they find themselves holding back. That isn't in our playbook for success. The coach got rid of that play and called an audible.

You can defeat fear with confidence. If you build up enough courage within you, you don't have to worry about fear. You will be able to look at every situation in the eye and do your best. Fear also comes from being pressured. Sometimes we put a lot of pressure on ourselves to deliver, and when we don't meet the goal or target, it translates into fear of getting back in and trying to step outside of our boundaries again. We become afraid of failing and this falls back into what makes us most comfortable, i.e., status quo. This should be a thing of the past with you. Be bold and confident knowing that you just have to do your best and leave the rest behind you.

Fear and doubt shouldn't have a place in your life if you want to succeed. I am able to put this book together because I overcame those negative emotions and doubts about my ability to truly write a book. Be secure in who you are and embrace your abilities knowing that you will get better with each passing day. This isn't something that you can change overnight, so practice continually and partner with someone who truly believes in you for support and guidance. Once you have fear and doubt in their proper place, we have to find out what success means to you individually and knock it out of the park.

CHAPTER EIGHT

DEFINE WHAT SUCCESS MEANS TO YOU

When tackling success, the most important thing we need to do is understand what success means to us individually. Success means different things to different people. You shouldn't measure your level of success with someone else's. What may seem like success to you may just be something fundamental to others, and what can be regarded as a success to someone else might not resonate with you. This creates a lot of issues for individuals primarily through the process of comparison. You look at the man over there and wish you had up to one-tenth of what he has, because what you see on the outside appears to emulate your personal definition of success. If you compare yourself to what another person has or does, you will always be aligned to his or her success and not your own.

So, I ask you at this point: What does success mean to you? What is it that can be ascribed to success for you? If you have an answer to this question, then you can comfortably say that you are on your way to victory. The internal definition is so important. It is one of the first things you should ask yourself if you want to avoid looking for someone to give you the definition of success, while you're in the midst of your journey.

You might be a sales representative and believe that success is hitting your sales goal in six months. With that in mind, you can put a plan in place as to how you can achieve this great accomplishment. The same goes for someone that says success for me is being a great father and friend. If you can't define what success means to you then you are always chasing a ghost, and nobody has done that, well since the ghostbusters. With this scenario in mind, you get to understand why it is so essential for you to clearly define what success appropriately means to you, so that you have a true gauge of your accomplishments.

When you know exactly what success means to you, it will help you to measure your progress. You are expected to measure your progress according to what you do and the circumstances surrounding the activities you carry out. Not based on someone else's estimation of the improvements you've made. When you define success to your standards, it gives you focus and helps you stick with them. If you own a restaurant and victory for you means your ability to open more restaurants within a particular zone, you will be so focused on this goal that nothing stops you.

I defined what success meant to me after the unfortunate incident I experienced. I realized that success for me is making an impact on others and helping people win in life. Ever since I started to take steps toward helping others to achieve their goals, I have felt a sense of success envelop me that it has become all I think about. Every day, I'm thinking of ways to make a difference in the lives of those around me. I don't look at the guy next to me and think,

"I should be as successful as that guy," because I have defined my success and I'm sticking to it.

Whatever you feel great at attaining is what success is for you. Whatever makes you feel good about yourself and increases self-worth is what success is to you. But you have to figure it out yourself, live on your terms, and don't allow anyone to dictate what success should mean to you. If you are focused on your journey, you will be much more efficient. Don't trade this for anything in the world. We are making a quick stop over at the boxing ring like Tony Johnson, Jr. so we can flex some muscles. You will learn how to fight back when life knocks you down. Get your boxing gloves ready. You're going to need them!

CHAPTER NINE

GET UP AND FIGHT BACK

You must have heard countless stories of people who were successful and then suddenly, they lost everything they had and couldn't make a comeback. Their story ended in an unfortunate, pathetic, and uninspiring way. The reason they couldn't make a comeback wasn't that they didn't know what to do. Instead, it was because they didn't put up a fight. They allowed the battle to overwhelm them to the point of not knowing what to do. You must never get to this point. In everything you do, always get set to put up a fight. "Failure is a bruise, not a tattoo," John Sinclair expressed and puts things into context. A tattoo is forever. It stays with you throughout your life. A bruise will heal. You may remember how you got it, but it no longer defines your identity.

The most successful people in the world, the ones you and I admire, have some of the most touching stories ever. They have stories of hurt, pain and significant loss. They didn't give up. They looked at the issues square in the eye and made a decision not to quit. It is crucial to build yourself up to this point. People who give up quickly have no story to tell. They do not inspire anyone, and there is no ounce of resilience in them. I recently listened to a Ted Talk and the feature was Brad Hurtig, a high school football player who did factory work on the side to earn extra money. While doing this, he lost both arms slightly under the elbow in a 500-ton power press. Most individuals would think that they would no longer be able to play football without hands. With the inspiration from his coach, Brad not only returned to play football, but he led his team in tackles and was an all-state linebacker. Initially, he had his doubts and fears that he would never be the same, but Brad got up and fought the doubt, fought the pain, fought the perceptions, and said, "try to stop me if you can." The next time you get knocked down, I want you to do the same.

I have shared my story with you throughout this book, and those who know me will tell you that I never take my boxing gloves off. None of us were born into this crazy world in defeat, and blood flows through our veins the same no matter who we are. If you see Goliath in your path, then you need to bring out the David in you, because it is your will to hunt down your dreams and win. My trainers and I set a goal for my recovery after the injury, a goal that made people think we were crazy. Most assumed that I would be lucky if I ever walked again without a limp. There was talk of shaving down the bones in my legs to straighten my gait, which in essence would have ended my ability to ever play sports again at a high level. Imagine hearing this as a freshman college student athlete.

The first true life decisions for me beyond deciding where to go to college, revolved around giving up the game that I loved, thus giving up a part of who I was. A couple of weeks into my rehab program, I was walking with my crutches to get breakfast on campus. There were no students in the cafeteria at this time because it was still summer break, and so it was me along with two or three teammates. I remember my teammate held the door so that I could get in because these were heavy glass doors with steel surroundings. I looked outside and saw that it had been raining, but I didn't think much about it, as I walked in and looked to crutch it to the line and get an omelet. I took one step in the door and placed my crutches down simultaneously trailing with my right leg. My injured left leg was bent and hanging in the air for protection, as I couldn't put weight on it for two months due to the trauma of the injury and the surgery. Click, click was the sound of crutches as they hit the floor—but something was wrong on this day. I felt my crutches sliding forward as if someone was wrenching them from my grasp. It was probably a split second, but it felt like a minute, as my heart quivered with fear. I lost my balance, and the only thing that I could do to not fall to the hard-ceramic tile floor was an auto-reflex. I caught myself with my injured leg, and before I realized what had just happened, the burning ring of fire exploded in my knee. The constant burn had finally gone away to some degree and now, because of a wet ceramic floor on a rainy day, I was submerged in unrelenting pain as my teammates rushed to my side to assure that I was okay.

A tear builds up as I am writing this. The memories are still fresh in my mind as if it all happened yesterday. My teammates immediately picked me up over their shoulders as I could not walk or move on my own at this point. The shock and pain shut down my ability to do anything. There were no cell phones since this was 1997, and the training room was a half mile away. Nobody knew what to do and there was panic all around. I heard a teammate say, "This isn't good," as I faded in and out of consciousness. The guys carried me all the way to training room on that hot September day. It was like in the movies as the group rushed me into the room and lay me on the table. Someone had run ahead to let Bill Walker know what was going on and he was waiting with his typical calm demeanor. But on this day, I knew something was wrong. Beyond the pain flowing throughout my body, everyone's face in the room painted a picture, and it wasn't pretty. I was rushed to UC Hospital for x-rays to check the graft and not even the cold x-ray table could numb the pain in my knee. Have you ever been in so much pain that your head is thumping like a heartbeat? This was the second time in 30 days for me and honestly, I am not sure which was worse. The doctor looked at the results and within 24 hours from the fall, I was prepped for surgery (the second one in a month). I was in my dorm room with Freddy Smith and JC Baker when my mom walked in that night, and it was the first time that I had broken down in front of my guys. I told my mom that I couldn't do this anymore. I don't know exactly what I meant with that statement as I write this today, but I can say that I wanted to be in another place, another body; out of this nightmare.

After the surgery, I broke down mentally and physically. The pain was excruciating. My will to fight was compromised and all I wanted to do was play football with my friends. Coupled with the pain, I wasn't eating. I started to lose weight and my momentum was gradually decreasing. I wanted to give up. But I knew deep down that I wasn't a quitter. I gave a loud scream as if I were in a horror movie to get the harmful toxins and thoughts out of my mind as I sat on the training table in the armory fieldhouse. We would rehab here so that the other athletes weren't distracted by my screams of pain, as I climbed the wall trying to escape Pat. She would sit on my back with a towel wrapped around my ankle. I was face-down and with all her might, she pulled my ankle as far as she could to my butt. You see, when I fell, I caused so much trauma that my entire knee scarred up as it attached to the original trauma like paper mâché. I almost lost flexibility in my leg had it not been for her dedication. We were never able to get complete flexibility back because of the severity of the trauma, but I found the resolve to pick up my gloves, get back up and fight. I haven't looked back since that day. It has been a battle to stay on top, to win and to be the best regardless of what may come my way, but I'm not going out without a fight no matter what the challenge is. You have the ability to do the same.

Sylvester Stallone once said, "You must fail a hundred times to succeed once." After every failure, you have to get back up and put in more intensity. The one time you win is worth more than the hundred times you failed. Nothing beats that feeling. This is why you have to fight. You have to try your very best to win against all the odds. If you are thinking about hanging your gloves and giving up as you read this, please make a U-turn and don't make such a colossal mistake. Had I not faced this challenge head on, I would be kicking myself today because I would always want to know, "could I have succeeded?"

You can enjoy your accomplishments better when you know that you have been through hell and still have what it takes to get back up and fight your way out. If you do this consistently when things go wrong or when adversity knocks on the front door, eventually it will be second nature. The next time it comes to knock in the future instead of hiding and lurking in the shadows, we will kick the door in and say, "try me if you wish!" Alright, now that we are fired up and ready to push full-speed ahead, we will learn how to adapt to any given situation. Sometimes you must bob and weave like MMA legend, Anderson Silva.

CHAPTER TEN

ADAPT

On your journey to success, you will be met with various experiences that bring you out of your comfort zone. It's okay to feel out of place initially, but don't stay too long in that mood. You need to adapt to any situation you find yourself in. A successful person looks beyond the immediate environment and makes an effort to be better. Let me say this: The road to success is bumpy and filled with a lot of adventure (poop). You will be amazed at all you will encounter and how far you go on your journey. I have adapted enough throughout my life that I feel like a farmhand, but it's worth it in the end.

The point is that you will be drawn out of what you thought was a comfortable position, and you have to come up with innovative ways through which you can deal with such unexpected occurrences. When I was a kid growing up, I attended six different schools before high school. Each move came with the uncomfortable first day where everyone wants to know who the new kid is. I was in the second grade when my mom, who was a young teacher, probably 28 at the time, received an offer to teach in Indianapolis. I had lived in Cincinnati all my life and pretty much within the shelter of Mayfair Drive. We lived with my late grandmother who was the love of my life. I was probably still sleeping in my grandmother's bed at night because first, the floor creaked and I thought the house was haunted; second, my mom would leave dresses hanging on the door. Close your eyes and go back to when you were seven years old. What does a dress on the back of the door look like in the dark? These are all excuses to validate my sleeping in granny's bed until second grade, but I will move on, as you get the point.

On the first day of school at Heather Hills Elementary, I walked in like a boss because that is what we are supposed to do after reading, "*22 Ways to Tackle Success*." I eyeballed potential friends, crushes and the classroom bully and settled in after the first hour or two. I heard the word "recess," and the room lit up like a Christmas tree with all those smiling faces. This was my type of class and these kids knew how to party! We lined up to head out, and Mrs. Webb let me walk with her. She knew I was still acclimating and could see that I hadn't jumped all in with the conversation just yet. We got outside and there was a foot of snow on the ground. I guess in Indiana they don't believe in indoor recess, but I was dressed for the occasion and ready to mingle. I peered out at my options as we got outside: 1. swing set; 2. tether ball; 3. kickball; 4. something unexplainable with all of the introverted kids. Kickball it is. It was a draft-style selection for the game and my confidence was high after I was picked up pretty quickly for the new kid. I was going to blow these kids away with my skills. The first time up to kick, I folded up my jeans so that I didn't get them wet, buckled my belt a hole tighter and I was ready to kick this ball back to Ohio. I saw it coming, I was picking my spot in the outfield over the head of my new crush, Amber. Here it comes—and bam! I completely missed the ball and my shoe went flying like a drone with a drunken pilot. I was blushing ear to ear by this time as I try to keep my foot with my sock off the ground when I heard "It's in the creek."

Calgon, take me away!

Day one at my new school and I missed the ball, kicked my shoe into a creek in the middle of winter and now the only solution was to wear Mrs. Webb's snow boots for the remainder of the day and the walk home. Talk about adapting quickly. The point is that I never envisioned moving to Indy and kicking my shoe so far in the creek that I had to wear my teacher's, but you know what? I had to adapt. Now, if you have a plan on how you want your career, business or whatever you're involved with to grow and you encounter some hiccups, don't spend a lot of time thinking about why such an incident is happening to you. Put on your teacher's shoes and keep going.

You must know how to adapt to spontaneous situations as well as work out strategies on how to manage them. I will be sharing some of the essential tips on how you can adapt to any situation, so you don't have to feel alone or left out when conditions overwhelm you. Ready?

Five Tips on How to Adapt to any Situation

1. Learn about the status

This should be your first response to a spontaneous situation. So many people start to panic even before they learn or try to understand the situation. When something happens, try to learn about it, try to understand it and don't be so quick to hit the panic button. Chances are that the process of getting to understand the situation will aid in easy assimilation of the issue.

2. Try getting used to the change

Oh, I had to get used to new students and pink snow boots all at the same time. It wasn't convenient for me, it wasn't easy and indeed not the best option, but I had to adapt. The next step to take after learning extensively about the situation, is to start getting used to the change. Do your best to work around it and try making it easy for you. Once you understand the situation and settle yourself into the new reality, you can now shift your mindset.

3. See the positive in everything

I am a confident person and I believe in being positive about everything that happens to me. Yes, it may be an unpleasant situation, but you have to see the good in everything. If you seek out the right in everything, you will experience excellent and positive energy. This is hard when adversity is bearing down on you, but it gets easier as you train and surround yourself with genuinely positive people.

4. Anticipate change

With spontaneous situations, comes change. It is inevitable. You will always encounter anxiety and stress when things like this happen, so don't be oblivious toward change. Embrace change and be optimistic about what is to come. The transition is still tough to handle, mainly when we are so used to a particular system or way of doing business, but you have to focus so that in the end, we have turned the change into a positive movement.

5. Move forward

After doing all that you can do, you should move forward. It wasn't an option to not go back to school and show my face. I had to bring Mrs. Webb her boots back and win friends in something less challenging than kickball on ice.

With these five steps, you will be able to handle whatever situations crop up at any time. Always remember to come back and refer to this, because what you have here applies to all scenarios and situations in life. The next phase of our journey is going to be even better. I know you've heard all about setting goals, but what about setting **GIGANTIC GOALS**? Let's begin, shall we?

CHAPTER ELEVEN

SET ASTONISHING GOALS

When I think about purposes, I am reminded of a gas station. You need to get gas so you can always be on the move, and you've got to go to the gas station to get gas, right? Your goals refer to the gas you need to give energy to your life. What is a human being without goals? You will drift through life wondering and thinking about your next move and not able to make sense of what you should be doing because you don't have goals. For one to succeed, goals must be set and strictly adhered to as it will determine a whole lot of things in the future. When I started out in my football career, my goal was to be the best, to be at the peak and to enjoy success because that was all I ever dreamed about.

With goals, you will be set on your way to properly strategize on how you can turn those goals into reality. However, I have observed that people place purposes and do not hit their targets. It can be frustrating to have goals and not make them work, which is why I will be sharing my top-five tips on useful goal setting that guarantee results. Goal setting for you will be positively different, and you will have a lot of fun seeing your goals come to completion. Let's begin with the top-five most effective ways to set and achieve goals.

Top-Five Most Effective Ways to Set and Achieve Goals

1. Plan

Before you set a goal, you must plan. Take a good look at your life and decide on what you want in exact and precise terms. When you start out with a plan, you shouldn't feel like you are making a mistake. Get a notepad, gather your thoughts and prepare for the future.

2. Set realistic goals

Your goals need to have elements of realism. You can't set goals that aren't achievable and expect magic to happen. For example, I can't be LeBron James, as I'm 40 and 5'10". It is essential that you look into your goals and ensure that there are things you can achieve. You want to be a superstar, then set gigantic goals that will aid to that, albeit realistically. Once your goals are realistic, achieving them will be nothing but a breeze as you integrate some of the 22 steps.

3. Use timelines

Goals will be achievable when you operate with timelines. If you have things to get done, you will respond to them promptly when you work with deadlines. After setting your goals, put a schedule with them and decide on when you intend to achieve them. You get a sense of urgency with timelines and it makes you get things done.

4. Measure your goals

You have to measure your goals from time to time. Don't get carried away with your timelines that you end up not checking on your goals. Regular checks help you ascertain how far you have come and what you need to do to get better. You can measure your goals by going through your plans again and checking your timelines.

5. Be consistent

Be consistent with your goals and you will never have to fall back in the achievement of your goals. Try to do precisely what you have said you will do, and you will get the right results. Be ready, be consistent, and be the best version of who you want to be. Goals can become a reality when you stay committed.

With the top-five tips outlined above, you can be sure that your goal-setting experience will be significantly different. You will be able to achieve more and make progress because it will be a time for significant improvement. The next chapter introduces the other type of fuel you will need for a successful life. We all need a little pain from time to time.

CHAPTER TWELVE

USE PAIN FOR FUEL

I know what it feels to live in pain. I'm 40 years old, and I can tell you when it will snow or rain by the ache in my body from my times on the gridiron. I was in so much pain during my traumatic events in college that I didn't want to take another breath in that state. This pain made me see all the things that had gone wrong in my life and all the aspects I didn't want to tolerate, yet I felt helpless. As I lay on the hospital bed, I couldn't stop thinking about the pain and what I can do to make it go away. Then it hit me. I saw a Michael Jordan quote that said, "My failure gave me strength; my pain was my motivation." Michael Jordan is to me is what LeBron James is to a lot of kids today. A living legend. When it came to sports, he was someone I looked up to. I grabbed my crutches, and I took one step out of bed and then another as I fought through tears. I reflected on my past. I thought about the great times I had with my teammates and relished my dream once more in my head, and you know what? At that moment, I decided that I was no longer going to focus on the pain through negative lenses. I decided to use the pain as a tool for regaining my dream. With every cry of agony from my knee rehab, I remembered all I wanted to achieve, and it propelled me forward even more.

I knew that there wasn't an athlete that we had seen at the time come back from this injury. I was determined to use the pain in my heart, my body and my mind, to become what my coach Rick Minter would eventually call, "a medical miracle." Sometimes pain is all you've got, and pain is all you need to make that shift from where you are to where you want to be. It begins with how passionate you are about what you want to achieve. When push comes to shove, you will be motivated through pain based on how inspired you are with the dream.

When you are faced with an impossible task, when something feels so painful, when you get to a place in your life where you aren't sure what happens next, use that feeling as fuel to activate your possibilities. Pain comes with a lot of discomfort. I remember feeling lost and alone after my struggles in the boardroom that I discussed in a previous chapter. But all of these feelings made it even easier for me to connect with my real passion and appreciate the little things in life.

Positivity can be derived from a negative situation, and you can make the most out of every condition you find yourself. This message of positivity is what success is about, and the sooner you start to embrace it the better for you. Get over the idea of being overwhelmed with pain and utilize it to make progress in life. Once you have a transformed mindset, the pain will no longer hurt. There will be physical manifestations of discomfort, but you will be triumphant in your mind because all you see is a success. You know it is your mind that matters. Once you win the battle in your mind, you can win in real life.

I thought the pain from my knee surgery was the worst pain that anyone could ever experience until I lost my best friend, my granny. The day that my granny passed away, I lost a part of me that I can never get back. I knew that I needed to honor her as best I could for the rest of my life. Everything that I do—from volunteering, to mentoring, to being the best man that I can be—was boosted from the pain that I experienced two years ago when granny passed. My actions and gratitude to service her memory live on, and she will always resonate in my soul.

Think of pain as a tool, a medium through which you get to inspire yourself, and you wouldn't have to think of the hurt that it brings. Remember that depression is a fuel. It isn't about what you feel; it's about what you do with the feeling. As we bring this chapter to a close, understand that whatever pain you might be going through or will go through will not be your end. You just have to look within and motivate yourself to greatness. The next chapter is all about you. You are the creator of your own success story. Believing in yourself is crucial to attaining greater heights.

I love you granny. Thank you for watching over me from above.

CHAPTER THIRTEEN

BELIEVE IN YOURSELF

E xperiences vary, and people can become a huge part of your story, but it doesn't mean that people's belief in you will cause you to succeed. You are the key player in your narrative. There is no one else but you in this great story of success. You owe it to yourself to believe and trust in who you are. I always use my account to inspire others because I think that my story is strategic in helping others to see how crucial it is for one to have faith in him/herself. You are confined only by the walls that you build for yourself in your head. Your ability to shoot for the stars is only possible if you give up the things that weigh you down. Doubt, fear, anxiety, age, and any other reason that we reach for to say, "I can't," will be replaced with confidence, belief, faith, and clarity.

Believing in yourself isn't negotiable. It is essential because it determines how far you will go. At some point, the world will turn its back on you. You will feel as though you are all alone and will have no one else to turn to. If you believe in yourself, that will suffice for as long as you want it to. To put it just: You are the most critical person in your story, and if you don't believe in your potential, then your journey will be marred by doubt and uncertainty.

The process of believing in oneself begins with looking beyond your immediate circumstances and not allowing the negative things you see, or experience keep you from seeing a better tomorrow. You are convinced about your journey and no one can tell you otherwise. The reason people lose faith in themselves is they allow the adverse circumstances they experience to drown the voice of success in their minds. What you say to yourself is crucial and if you have built confidence in your abilities, then you shouldn't be moved by anything contrary. I am a big believer in affirmations, after it was mentioned to me by a coach of mine. I am confident, knowledgeable, genuine and kind. I am a valuable communicator, connecting people to what they need. These are the affirmations that I choose for myself. I have an 8x11, laminated copy at my desk, highlighted in black and red. What I want you to do is look up positive affirmations and create something specific to you and your opportunities. I believe in you and that you can do anything.

Your story of success will be complete when you look back and realize that despite all odds, you didn't give in. Think about this: Would I have a story to share with you if I had given up and never took the field again without trying? Do you think it would have been possible for me to put a book together if I stopped believing in myself when they said I may never walk again without a limp? From this analysis, you get to understand that believing in yourself works for both you and the people who look up to you. Our perspective on success shouldn't be one-sided. We shouldn't be focused on what is in it for us alone, but on those who experienced worse situations than what we might have gone through.

Success is akin to getting what you've always wanted after going through life's compulsory process, but the beautiful thing about success lies in the fact that you can get what you want without having to lose sight of who you are. Look in that mirror and tell yourself whatever you want. You are the architect of your own life and if you don't take charge now, you might lose that power. Don't let someone else determine your story. Believing in yourself when the chips are down is always challenging and, sometimes, you just want to throw in the towel and forget about trying. But, hold on for a moment. It is in times like this you should never give up. The more you survive the challenging times, the stronger you get. A wrestler has to go through the rigorous process of training and cutting weight just to prepare for a match. In the process of training he may get hurt, break a limb or a finger. However, after the hellacious process, he will be prepared for his opponent and no matter how vast this opponent is, the wrestler will always believe in himself because he has trained and prepared for this moment.

Your challenging phase is a training ground. Don't take it for granted and don't give up midway. Train on and get better with each passing day. You are building faith in yourself and believing in your abilities. Paying attention to details and working smart are additional aspects to success you must consider all the time. Let's find out more.

CHAPTER FOURTEEN

PAY ATTENTION TO DETAIL; WORK SMART

Have you noticed that successful people tend to pay the most attention to detail about everything in their life? It has already been established here that success is a process, and a vital aspect of that process includes you paying close attention to the things you do. It goes beyond work, job and business. It cuts across every aspect of your life in general. Your ability to place even the tiniest detail into place makes you exceptional. When you pay attention to detail, it also helps you to work extra smart. There is a thin line between being excellent and mediocrity, and you can get rid of that line by paying close attention to detail.

In this chapter, we are going to consider the aspects of life we haven't looked at in a while, and this covers your personal life. It is so easy to talk about success and focus on work, job, business or career and completely forget about your own life. However, I believe that success should be a balanced art. You shouldn't sideline any aspect of your life. Paying attention to detail shouldn't be just at work, but in your life as well. I will consider the work aspect because that's what you are used to and then walk you through success from the perspective of personal life.

Beginning with work, you can pay attention to detail by taking note of every aspect of your responsibility, e.g., from the type of paper you use to print, the products you retail, your office space, and how quickly and professionally you respond to emails and the people around you. Are you professionally memorable to others? If you tend to go to the office, engage with your mobile device and are not being conscious of your environment, you need to start by changing that. Be present with your work and business. Be attuned to your activities and you will observe that there is a significant amount of progress in your life. I relish in doing thing differently to a point where others want to know my process and routine. That's when you are doing things the right way at a high level. I will say that I am not a natural at this, so I bring in help because I know how important it is to my success.

Some of the mistakes you make that set you back can be avoided if you focus on the details. Think back to the times you felt like you didn't get something right. You probably thought you should have done better, right? Well, that feeling stems from the fact that you should have paid attention to and prepared better for what you were supposed to do. Its why athletes practice moves over and over before the game. Its why artists work tirelessly to perfect their craft. In your work, pay better attention. It will enable you to work smarter and help add value to the things you do.

Now, let's talk about your personal life. You see, when you place value on your life and the people around you, your friends and family and the ones who matter the most, it makes you pay attention to detail. If you are going to be successful, you need to take them with you on that journey. When was the last time you went to a Parent Teacher Association meeting? A ballet recital? Have you visited your parents in a while or checked in on Aunt Shirley? I know that some of you do a great job of this on a daily basis, but there is always room for us to grow in this area of life. These moments make all the difference at the end of the day. When I was at my lowest point in life after tearing my ACL again with the New York Giants, my family stood by me and knew that I would overcome once again. They were there to hold my hand through it all because over time, I paid attention to their well-being and gave all that I had. Personal relationships can be difficult. If we aren't rightly grounded in our professional and personal lives, we can have a see-saw effect. When this occurs, we find it difficult to keep personal and professional success at a high level. Every time I win at one, the other takes a dip.

Pay attention to your personal life and the people you care about the most. You will be planting seeds of love that will germinate into fantastic family experiences later on. Your stability in life hinges on your ability to manage both personal and work-related issues. Once you strike a balance, you can weather any storm in life. Paying attention to detail is excellent for success, and it aids in working smartly.

CHAPTER FIFTEEN

LISTEN! THINK BEFORE YOU ACT

I n the previous section, I referred to listening as a skill. A lot of people spend time talking, giving out orders, and being in charge of things. However, when you learn how to listen, you gain insight into things and can solve problems or provide solutions. In all areas of your life, try to be a good listener. Listen to the people trying to get your attention, to your inner voice and to the things around you. In the course of my career, I have had instances where I had to take a breather and listen. Those were defining moments for me, because as an athlete, I was always coming forward taking charge. In business, those who listen and learn will gain great insights that can be used to win if utilized strategically. From the time I meet someone, I begin listening to the words coming out if his or her mouth, the way that they are expressing them, the mannerisms they display. Pulling all of this data together to utilize in many ways for good. There are sometimes it's great as well because you know when to run when you find a bad apple.

We live in a fast-paced world full of action, movies, and fast food. We are always quick to respond before listening. This fast-paced life has caused more harm than good to our communication style. So now we have individuals who go out of their way to act before they gain understanding. There are various aspects to listening, and you will be learning these different elements as we go on in this chapter.

First, you've got to know how to listen to yourself before you act. This is so important. That voice in your head is your best bet at making some of the best and some of the worst decisions in life. If you have been training your mind in the right direction, then the voice you hear in your head will never lead you astray. Before you take that huge step, before making that decision, you have to listen to yourself. If you act before listening, the mistakes you make will haunt you. During senior year in high school, my head coach was playing scout team quarterback and we were intercepting him left and right. I yelled out, with all the confidence in the world, "Nice throw Bernie!" thinking of the Cleveland Browns' Bernie Kosar. By the time I realized that it was an awful idea, as our coaches name was Bernie Barre, I had the wrath of one angry coach coming my way. I think he was shocked more than anything because for me to say something like that was totally out of my character. Unfortunately, I didn't listen to that voice inside my head saying "bad idea" before I opened my mouth. Be patient with yourself by listening to you. That voice is light. It will guide you. If it's guiding you in the wrong direction, we have to change the mindset of the voice.

Next, you need to listen to the voice of experience. Come on. You have experience running your business and life, and you know that history often repeats itself. When you have a decision to make, look back at your life. Chances are, you may have faced such a tough decision before and won. Rather than make a hasty decision, you should listen to what experience has to say and make a decision in line with that. Your experience will give you a better perspective and help you act in the right stead. Don't underestimate the power of your experience. Another element of this is to listen to the experience of others. I have a consultant at work who has the biggest client base in the company and has excelled for years as a leader in the industry. You better believe I asked how he not only created success but maintained it. Listen to experience, and you won't have to completely reinvent the wheel.

You should also listen to the voice of professionalism. This is one voice I always listen to when I need direction in life. The professional view will help you act in your own best interest, thus ensuring that you make decisions that will allow you to maintain professional integrity and be respected among your family and peers. In other words, acting right in your business, job, or career will set you on the path to success.

Learn how to listen to the experts before you act. I had to listen to my doctors. They were the experts; they knew what needed to be done to make things right. Despite the fact that I was in pain and had my own agenda, I had to listen to what the experts said and acted accordingly. It's natural to feel like we are the pilots of our life and thus have all the answers, but you can get ahead in life when you listen to the people who have more knowledge about your field or where you are looking to go in life. Do not make efforts without adequately gaining insights into what you should do beforehand.

The skill of listening will serve you for a very long time. Be a great listener and you will be able to go farther. Listening and acting go hand in hand. You work after you hear not before, so be sure that you have the correct information before you take that leap. If you flip to the next chapter, you will discover the important roles that other people play on your journey to success.

CHAPTER SIXTEEN

SURROUND YOURSELF WITH OTHER SUCCESSFUL PEOPLE

L ook around you because the people that you surround yourself with will have an impact on how successful you will be in life. The statement above isn't a cliché; it is a fact. If you are surrounded by mediocre people, then you will be average as well. If you are surrounded by excellent individuals, you will indeed be excellent. As simple as this evaluation is, so many people haven't gotten it. There is something about the energy that surrounds you, it can make or mar you. I learned about this secret to success a long time ago through experience; hence, I became extra careful with the company I kept. If you look back at your life you will discover that some of the issues, challenges, and successes you had, were in more ways than one, related to the people you had around you at the time.

I became a success mainly because of the people who had such a massive influence in my life. I didn't grow up with my dad, as I lived with my mom, but his presence was always there. I missed the daily father–son teachings due to our distance but I was still able to extract a work ethic, commitment, and determination from him. My father works more than anyone that I have ever met, and if I text or call, he is still always there. Not wanting to let him down pushes me to greatness, as I want him to be proud of me as I am of him.

I have a plethora of teammates that I speak with daily. JC Baker is engaged in many projects from tech to business consulting all over the country. Rob Lucas and his wife have created an empire and their success pushes me to continue to grow. Troy Evans played ten years in the NFL after our time with the Bearcats, and he now has one of the fastest-growing companies in the medical field. From successful teammates to influential coaches, I enjoyed the company of successful people; their ideas, belief systems and confidence rubbed off on me. I have had the opportunity to learn from Rex Ryan, Mike Tomlin, John Harbaugh, Jimbo Fischer, Greg Hudson, and others that I have noted in this book. These guys were great coaches. They focused on ensuring that we knew how to be a professional man outside of the lines. I had such a fantastic mindset toward life, ready to take on significant new challenges because the people around me never stopped pushing the boundaries. They inspired me to greatness and made it so easy for me to dream big dreams.

You see my life had a great twist because these people made life better. I am blessed to be surrounded by great people today, but you have to be open to making a change. Robert Cooper is my best friend in this world today, but it didn't start that way. When we were recruited to The University of Cincinnati, there was a magazine that highlighted the incoming class. I had one whole page on the left, and "Super Cooper," as they described him, had one on the right. I was on defense and he was on offense as a running back. From the day that we met, we fought like cats and dogs—not from a street-fight standpoint but from a competitive standpoint. On the field, in the weight room, picking up ladies, to the 40-yard dash, we were aligned from that magazine to compete to be the best. I can honestly say that he made me a better player and we gained such a mutual respect for each other through this competition, that we have been able to transition this mentality to life.

If you are always surrounded by the wrong people, then your life will be a reflection of what these people believe in. With negative people come negative energies, and this will keep you in a wrong space until you make a change. Take a good look at your circle occasionally and fish out those who aren't helping you get anywhere in life, but rather bringing you down. Locate them out and cut them off. You don't have to create a scene or go all out and be nasty. Just cut them out and move on. I had to get out of a personal relationship because I began to absorb her negative energy. I'm a doer and she is a dreamer. I'm a grinder and she prefers status quo. I'm a perfectionist and she is okay with gray. In respect for your mental health and your ability to achieve success at the highest level, make sure your partner is aligned with your goals. It's a beautiful thing.

Successful people will make you better in every way. They are a constant source of inspiration and they should fuel your motivation whenever you are around them. You can count on them at all times, learn from them, and build a great relationship with people who add value. I have a mentor and friend in Randy Church, which made a huge difference in my life without even realizing it. He asked me to coach his son's first-grade football team with him, and after my initial hesitation due to their age, I was all in. Imagine these little bobble heads running around with pads bigger than their bodies, and I was there trying to install the Rex Ryan 46 defense. I wound up coaching these kids from the first grade until they left for middle school and it was one of the greatest experiences of my life. The kids, the parents, the coaches all mean so much to me, and it started with a simple invitation from Randy because he knew how passionate I am about helping.

If you want to have a success story, then get close to people who already reached where you are looking to go. The beautiful thing about this resides in the fact that you've got successful people all around you—in your industry, workplace, line of business, career, etc. Look out for those who are exactly where you want to be and model your life after theirs in your own way.

Success always leaves clues. If you follow the trail, you will discover that your story can be just how you want it to be. You just need to follow the same pattern laid out by successful people before you. There will be times when you are faced with challenges you never envisioned and you are swarmed with all kinds of thoughts, wondering how you can make it. In those times, you can draw strength from the amazing people around you. You can bring power and lessons from those who have gone ahead of you in the areas you are just trying to break into.

You will never feel lost in the world if you have the right people around you. You will always be one step ahead all the time because successful people want to see you succeed also. Regardless of my travails, I still had that inner confidence that everything will be all right; after all, I had the right people to look up to and gain inspiration. Surround yourself with successful people and you will be on your way to success. As we move on, we will learn how to leave the past behind, as we look forward to the future with hope and a renewed commitment toward success.

CHAPTER SEVENTEEN

DON'T LIVE IN THE PAST

Everyone has a past, present, and future. It is just a part of the life cycle. History refers to the aspect of being behind you; the current is right where you are now; and the future is where you are going. These three phases shape the events that take place in your life and always keeps the circle moving. However, you've got to know what to do at every phase, so you can maximize the timing. In this book, we are talking much about things that you can do in your present state to attain success in the future. The only time you should look back at your past is to see how far you have come because, when our phases collide with each other, it's usually a disaster to our current momentum. Zig Zigler once said, "How you see your future is much more important than what has happened in your past." This quote exemplifies what we have discussed throughout this book. Our train is moving forward, and we left the rearview mirrors at the station.

The focus of this chapter is your past and why you should no longer live there and some of the consequences of when we do. People becomes engrossed in the history of their lives, especially when they've had it good for a while. When things go wrong in the present, they wish they were back in a certain period of time, back at previous job, or possibly back with a spouse or partner. I strongly disagree with this assertion particularly because there haven't been many examples of when this has helped someone succeed in the present. A majority of time those that do chase that ghost behind them tend to repeat the same bad cycle and replicate the result, only to find themselves back at ground zero.

Knowing how to strike the balance is crucial to living a successful life. I know that I keep repeating this, but it's so important. You have to put the past where it belongs and bury it, especially if you are one to ponder like I described above. Now, there were days when I couldn't stop myself from looking back to my real estate days and how easy life seemed to be—the boats, the cars, pretty beaches, and fast money. It was a real struggle for me early on after I had to restart my career after the mortgage collapse. I was sitting in a nine-to-five with no boat, no pretty beaches, snow, a crappy salary and a boss. This sense swallowed me in until I had nothing else to think about. Talk about a reality check. With time, I realized that I was tainting my own ability to find happiness by letting the past do jumping jacks in my brain. I looked at my dwindling bank account from debts of the past, and that assured me that history is where it needs to be. Why reach for it and cast doubt on my current state? Whatever you thought you achieved in the past can be better in the future even when starting back at zero. The mistakes of the past can be corrected, and you can build even better strategies. You just need a little patience and be willing to fight.

There is a massive difference between reminiscing, which you will see in a lot of the stories shared about my own past and being nostalgic about it. When you reminisce, you think back to time and analyze the history; however, nostalgia means you want to go back to the past, and this is where the problem lies. Nobody wants to pay $39.99 to see 2018 DeJuan Gossett play safety for the Bearcats today—maybe my mom. However, there are many people out there who would love to see 2018 DeJuan Gossett make plays tackling success in life, and they are willing to help along the way. If there is one thing you must never hold onto, it is the past. One of my favorite things to say is, "I am going to make the rest of my life the best of my life." I don't have time to look back when I'm focused on building something better in the future.

With everything you have learned thus far, be reminded that the past is gone. It is never coming back. The future is way ahead of you, but the present is now. You can only get one shot at present. Take it and run with it. Communication is needed if you are going to be successful, and it's one of my favorite chapters because I love to talk. Let's put the past in the rear-view and get started.

CHAPTER EIGHTEEN

COMMUNICATE

The power of communication cannot be denied in your quest to gain success. Communication makes it easier for ideas to be shared; as such, it makes the world better. More so, everyone wants to be heard. You like to be heard, don't you? I know I do. Communication is key. The connection is a two-way street, there's you at one end and then the other person(s). For you to gain access to certain things in life, you will have to speak up at some point. This chapter reveals the role communication plays to achieve success. Without making a connection, it is difficult to make progress. Learning how to communicate correctly is key in going forward.

There are three sides of communication: the sender, the message and the receiver. The sender is the person who speaks, the word is what is said, and the receiver is the person who is spoken to. These elements are present every time you communicate, so look out for them and ensure that you play your part. Now I am going to share my top-seven tips on how you can efficiently communicate.

These steps will help you to maintain a communication pattern that enables you to deliver quality communication at every turn. Are you ready to explore these tips? Read on.

My Top-Seven Tips for Effective Communication

1. **Listen.** The first thing about discussion is that you have to listen. Listen to the person you're talking to and listen to the person who is talking to you. It's that simple. When you listen, you will be able to pick up details of the communication process. Do not listen with closed ears as you prepare to speak in response. Listen to learn, and your response will resonate with your subject.

2. **Be Precise.** If you are going to be a success, then you have to be precise with your words. Choose your words carefully and be sure to stay conscious throughout the conversation. When you are correct, you will not be misquoted or misunderstood. I tend to get wordy as I am passionate about getting my point across, so always in the back of my mind I am aware and condensing my message with precision.

3. **Share your thoughts.** As you communicate, it is essential that you share your thoughts. Don't hold back because you feel your ideas will not be appreciated or received, because being bold is an attribute successful people embody. Say what you want to say and worry about nothing.

4. **Ask questions.** When you converse with a person or a group, ask questions when you feel lost. Many people just allow words to slip by them and do not seek clarity. At the end of the day, they end up doing the wrong things because of a lack of transparency. Focus on open-ended questions and if you never know what to ask. Prepare a list of five to ten

questions and learn them like the back of your hand. They will roll off of your tongue and possibly put you at ease in conversation.

5. **Recognize communication barriers.** There are barriers to communication and as you communicate, you have to be able to identify those obstacles and squash them. The person you speak to might exhibit signs that interrupt the communication process, and if those restrictions are not correctly handled, communication will not be sufficient. There are many times where I will ask to reschedule or wait in silence if someone seems distracted. If you do not have the full attention of your audience, you may be wasting your breath.

6. **Focus on the business at hand.** If you are communicating with business, then focus on that. If it is for leisure, then do the same. The focus is crucial as it helps you keep the discussion on track.

7. **Speak openly.** This is so important. The people you speak to should hear you, so no whispering and hasty assumptions that someone can listen to you when you have been talking to yourself the whole time. If you see the subject coming forward with a tilted head, he or she most likely cannot hear you. If you don't feel that you come through crystal clear on the phone, then stand up. It will do wonders.

These seven tips come in handy for all conversations. Your level of communication will significantly improve when you take these tips to heart. Start by listening before you speak. Be concise and precise with your words and always share your thoughts. Asking questions also help because you will be able to recognize communication barriers such as being inaudible. If you speak enough, the flow of communication will never cease. Grab a recorder and record yourself. Play it back, and know this is what you sound like to your audience. If you do not like what you here, then practice. I promise you will get better and be more confident in your delivery.

CHAPTER NINETEEN

GIVE BACK: MENTORSHIP

Whatever kind of success you have attained right now can be traced back to the influence someone had over you. In some ways, you have received a form of mentorship from someone, so you should be ready to give back. As I sat down in my office thinking about my journey thus far, I thought about the best ways through which I could give back beyond my board commitments and volunteerism. The thought was so overwhelming; it propelled me into putting this book together and increasing my participation with local nonprofits in the greater Cincinnati community. You can find a link to some of them on my website at www.22wtts.com.

You can give back wherever you are from. Through mentorship, you can make a massive investment in the life of someone. If you can replicate your successes through mentoring, you can make the most out of your experience by sharing all you know with someone who is on their way to becoming like you. Mentoring is such a beautiful experience. It helps you to see yourself through the eyes of someone else and keeps you grounded on the things you feel you already know. If you have reached a certain height in your career, business, or professional life, it's time to give back. It's time to reach out to someone and add value to his or her life.

So how do you mentor an individual? What are the steps to take? What can you do? As much as the idea of mentoring sounds fun, you need to be sure that you know exactly what you are doing. It won't be a pleasant experience if you lead someone into thinking you can teach him or her certain things about life, and then you aren't able to live up to those expectations. To mentor someone, you have to be sure that you are ready to share all that you know and indeed make an impact.

Being a mentor also means you are willing to put others first. You will be partnering with this person and putting their needs into perspective. He or she is a sponge waiting to learn from someone like you. I have a lot of experience mentoring others and if you are willing to learn, then you will benefit from one of the most selfless, fulfilling experiences you will ever have. Don't worry! It's going to be so much fun.

- **Identify the Purpose of Mentoring**

    This is the first step to take in mentoring. What are your mentoring goals? Why do you want to mentor? What's your vision? These questions will help sharpen your focus and make it easier for you to decide on who you want to mentor.

- **Cultivate a Relationship**

    After identifying your purpose, you need to cultivate a relationship with your mentee. Your mentoring sessions shouldn't be about growing alone but sharing a bond that is both professional and personal. This will aid the bonding process.

- **Schedule Mentoring Sessions**

  Mentoring sessions are opportunities for you to have time with your mentee(s). Your mentoring sessions can be at a time and place agreed upon by you and your mentee(s), and such meetings will help you measure your progress.

- **Commitment**

  Mentoring is about being committed to the process of transforming a person. It doesn't matter how long it takes for you to make a difference. Stay true to the person, and the process and you will reap great rewards.

- **Patience**

  You have to be patient. Oh, yes. Patience is a virtue concerning mentoring, and if you see your mentoring efforts through to the end, you will be amazed at the level of fulfilment and satisfaction you derive from seeing the transformation of another individual.

I have shared the best tips you need to become a fantastic mentor. I am sure you will make a huge impact with these steps. It doesn't take much for you to become a great mentor. Just have faith in your ability to mentor and believe in the individual(s) you intend on mentoring. Ready to mentor now? We will have more information on mentoring programs on our website if you have questions. It's our goal to create awareness all over the country and to build an army of successful people like you in helping others to achieve their goals and dreams.

If mentorship does not interest you, there are so many more ways to give back. This year, I spent an entire day at summer camp with campers from Stepping Stones, in Cincinnati. This organization has been helping people with disabilities find pathways to independence since 1963. The experience was phenomenal. It's one where you feel guilty when you leave, because I may have gotten more from those campers that day than I could possibly give to them.

You may ask how a book about success culminates to a chapter on giving back and mentorship. I promise you that one common theme among successful individuals is their willingness to give back and help others. It's not 100% as nothing is, but in my heart, I feel that it is important. I want you to start thinking about it no matter where you are in life. The easiest way to tackle success beyond starting now, is to be a good person. Good people have the soul of an angel and bring joy into the hearts of others with just their presence. It's something that we can all attain no matter our age, sex, creed or religion.

If you would like the opportunity to be aligned with a mentor near you, please reach out at www.22wtts.com.

CHAPTER TWENTY

ORGANIZATION: PLAN/PREP

A successful person is organized. It is true that successful individuals take their time to plan and set things in order before they embark on any journey or task. I'm going to spend time sharing the importance of organization, planning and prepping for any activity in work, or life in general. Being organized starts by recognizing the fact that disorganization is something that cannot survive in an environment of success for most people.

I believe that when you are organized, you set the way for greater opportunities to fall into place for you. It's like setting up the chain for successive victories. Your level of organization will always make it possible for you to do more and share more efficiently. Have you taken a real look at life recently? Are you convinced that you are on the right track, doing what needs to be done, when it's supposed to be done, and how it's supposed to be done? Or are you like most individuals today who are flying by the seat of the pants hoping to land without a crash?

So, you have got to be organized. From work to home and then your business, think about what you need to be doing to learn and expand your reach. Plan your events, the people you should meet with, places to go, and how you intend on getting there. Planning contributes to making life so much easier for you. As you plan, you'll realize that when you wake up in the morning, you have already laid out what you need to accomplish. You cannot be a success without being someone who plans, because you need a clear mind to take on this big goal that we are going to have you tackle.

Before presenting the finished product of this book, I had to plan and strategize on the best ways through which you the reader, can have a great experience during and after reading it. My organization of things have paved the way for what I hope, is a great book. It has become the blueprint of many and is one of the reasons why people are encouraged about success. You can achieve a whole lot just by planning. It saves time, makes it easier for you to make a decision, and helps in bringing out the best in you. Every Sunday, I put my suits together for the week with a shirt-and-tie combination. I ensure that I don't have angst in the morning as I come into work and I can focus on what I need to do for my clients so that we can achieve success. After meetings, I send recaps so that the meeting is fresh in my head and others have clarification on the next steps. These are all things that are a part of my planning routine to ensure that I have a clear mind to chase success. Find out what works for you and your specific needs and be fanatical about it. I promise it will be a benefit. If you cannot stick to it on your own, recruit an accountability partner and make it fun. You will see instant results.

I have met people who experienced life in a haze, not knowing what to do next, not being sure of anything, and just being confused about life. This isn't an attribute you will find in successful people. Make planning a significant part of your life by scheduling and putting everything into time segments. I have given countless reasons why you should plan, why you have to stay organized and prepared because planning helps bring thoughts into reality, and it shapes the way I view things, people, and life in general. You will be an entirely different person when you plan. The person who doesn't plan is always scattered, has excuses all the time, and never meets up in time for meetings. On the other hand, the person who is organized gets the most business deals done and has a reputation for excellence. Who do you think will experience success more? The latter guy, of course!

Begin to cultivate the attributes of planning and being an organized person now. You can start with smaller responsibilities; then, as you get used to planning them, you gradually move it up to more significant responsibilities. Just be sure that you are continually planning and staying organized. I look forward to getting fantastic success stories from you as you implement the steps provided in this book. In fact, you will need to plan and organize yourself toward doing precisely what has been shared. The next chapter is about the role of your health in helping you attain success. Read on and get to work!

CHAPTER TWENTY-ONE

HEALTH AND WELLNESS

Your health is your wealth, and if you have any intentions on being successful and sustaining it, you need to ensure that the pilot of your future (YOU) is the best you that you can possibly be. Even if you were able to miraculously make big things happen while abusing your mind, body, and soul along the way, the percentages are against you in regard to continuing with the energy and vigor you will need to sustain your goals. To put it simply, without being healthy, you cannot be your best you. You need to be in the top form filled with health and vitality and having the strength to do all that you want to do.

When I changed positions to a top-executive role, the first thing that I did was engulf myself into my work. You could find me in the office at 6:30 a.m., and you could guarantee that I would be there when the cleaning crew arrived at 7 p.m. I skipped breakfast, only ate lunch if I had a prospect meeting, and to relax I would grab dinner on my way home at the local pub along with a drink, or possibly seven. I would wake up the next day and do it all over again, but I found myself hitting a wall and didn't understand why. I wasn't killing it with results like I felt that I should. My suits started to shrink as my butt started to expand, and I was getting grouchy at home after a long day. Have you ever had this happen? What I tried to do was completely counterproductive to who I need to be to climb the highest mountain daily. I was depriving my body of nutrients. I wasn't fueling my metabolism by working out to give me the energy for those long nights in the office, and I was fatigued to the max. A recipe for disaster. The first question that my accountability coach asks if I start to fall with production is "Are you taking care of yourself'?

In your pursuit of success, you have to take the time to check your health status and ensure that you are healthy on the inside and outside. Do you feel like you are ready to take on all of the activities required of you? Are you eating well enough? If you don't take the time to ask these questions, you might end up with a flawed body system that is unable to take the heat that comes with mounting a lot of pressure on yourself to succeed.

Success is complete when you are healthy. You are at the very peak of success when you can do all that is required of you from a healthy state of mind. It is akin to being at rest, yet you can do several things that enhance success. The journey to health and wellness has multiple facets, and as we go on in this chapter, we will unveil these aspects and discover how you can indulge in them and maximize your time correctly.

The first aspect to consider when talking about health and wellness is the kind of food you eat. You get nutrients from food; as such, if you are eating properly, you will experience a surge of nutrients and energy that keep you vitalized. So, I try to get more protein into my diet, fewer carbs, eat breakfast, drink lots of water, and avoid eating junk meals as much as possible. My body is my temple. I ask employees all of the time why would they put discount fuel into their bodies when they wouldn't do the same to their cars. In order to be the best you, you have to start treating yourself as the best. Once you get your dietary part right, you can be sure that every other thing will build on it and make your journey to success an exceptional one.

Next is exercise. Your body has to get familiar with movements and routines that aid blood circulation as well as contribute to strengthening your cells. Medical experts say that stagnation is the new smoking. Register with a gym, take the stairs to work, and skip the elevator. Go for morning walks and engage an account-ability partner to keep you on track. Always be in motion. I am on the move constantly with work. I have four gym memberships so that I cannot make an excuse when it comes to location. These exercise routines will not only strengthen you but will help you to create a pattern that encourages you to always keep fit. As much as an athlete that I was, I am the worst when it comes to cardio, but I realize how important it is for my heart. I join classes where I am pushed by others. This may be the death of me, as I am the most competitive individual alive, and there is this fit girl in the class who is dynamic. I try to beat her in drills every day but to no avail. I will succeed, however. I know what my shortcomings are, and so I put myself in a position to fuel my strengths. You need to do the same—and you must.

With exercise and good food, you are on your way to getting bet-ter days, but there is one more thing you can do to aid health and wellness: Get regular checks with your primary care physician. You've got to always check your body and vital organs periodically, just to be sure that everything works perfectly just as you would your automobile. By doing this, you give no room for catastrophic events, and you stay one step ahead health-wise. All new cars have "check engine" lights and "service now" alerts. We do not have chips yet as humans, so grab a calendar and your phone. Schedule your yearly physical with your primary care physician, then schedule a dental exam and a vision exam. If you do these three things, you will be ahead of a majority of people in this country, and that is scary. I have seen many clients implement a primary care physician requirement and have employee's begrudgingly go the doctor. They are usually guys by the way, as we can complain about anything not sports-related. The results are always telling in that I hear that people are looking to make a change and that the culture of the company is changing. I ask why, and the answer is that people are "aware." If you knew your hair was in danger of catching on fire, would you want to know and take steps to ensure that it doesn't? The answer is always going to be "yes." The problem is that too many of us don't know that our hair is on fire until it's too late. Don't be a statistic. Being healthy and maintaining wellness are things anybody who wants to be successful should take seriously. You cannot make groundbreaking innovations when you are battling with one illness after the other. Take great care of yourself first and every other thing will fall in line. Taking the first step is always crucial to gaining results and the next chapter x-rays the importance of starting out early. Enjoy the read.

CHAPTER TWENTY-TWO

START NOW

The easy part is over as we are coming to an end of this ride. I am incredibly proud of you for making it this far. Some people begin a book and cannot make it halfway because they lack the determination to stay strong and finish its entirety. Some people will stop reading if the topic or author doesn't resonate with them. You started out well, coasted through the middle of the game and now we are ending the fourth quarter. This is the section where legends are born, and it's all about you and your desire to be the best you. Every major quarterback that we hear about in GOAT conversations, comes alive in the fourth quarter when the pressure mounts. It's put up or shut up. The stories I shared with you, the concepts of success, the examples and contributions I made, what are you going to do with all of this information? It is one thing to read a book, and another thing entirely doing what you encountered in the book.

I always admonish individuals I come across who have read several books but don't have significant results to show for the knowledge they acquired to be more of doers than readers. It is good to understand, but what's even better is what you do with the knowledge that you have retained. It takes us back to the quote we noted in Chapter 6: "Happiness is in the doing and not in getting what you want." I want to add to that and proclaim that "players make plays." It doesn't matter if you know what to do, understand what to do, or even have a passion about you're doing, if you don't take the most important step, which is to squash the status quo and Start Now! This chapter aims at pushing some of us out of our comfort zones. I used to be the biggest procrastinator until I got tired of having great ideas, thoughts, dreams and wishes. I've learned through my life that nothing comes without action, so today its 4th and 10 and the ballgame is on the line. Buckle your chinstrap, put your mouthpiece in and tackle your dreams. Do not let another moment slip away.

Let's back up for a second as we get ready to close with this game-changing stop. Go back to the first chapter and remind yourself of everything we talked about. As you go through the sections, take note of the areas where you need to take action and write them down in permanent marker. If you need to get a nutritionist to help out with your meals, make a note to do that; if you need a mentor, start the process of getting one. Whatever you want to do must begin right now because now is the best time. If you don't know where to find resources in your area, reach out at info@22wtts. com, and one of our team members will help.

The one thing I love about sharing my knowledge with others, is getting testimonies of how the concepts that I shared, helped in shaping a life. It is the most fulfilling aspect of writing. Just like every other experience I've had to speak and share my story, I look forward to hearing how you have made progress in life and tackled fear, doubt, fatigue, marriage, disappointment, and rejection along the way. You will only be as good as the things you do and the steps you take, so don't hold yourself back with inactions. Activate what you know by doing what needs to be done. These negative things are coming to take your joy, and I know that anyone who has come this far on this journey with me is going to stand up and fight back. I also revel in the success of others. If you have more steps that you would like to share, let us know at the blog for *22 Ways to Tackle Success*. This is a team effort, and we had to stop at 22 because it's the best number in sports, of course.

I promise that you will be grateful for this journey, if you make the journey a part of your life by implementing all that you have learned in this book. It is a fantastic experience, growing I mean, because success is synonymous with growth. The only way for you to ascertain if you are building is by checking the things you do on a daily basis. So be productive, be deliberate, and become the best version of who you want to be because it is possible. I believe in you. I am committed to your success. Don't hold back! Give it your all, and you will be great.

Fourth and 10 ... game is on the line. What are you going to do to tackle success? (If you purchased this book, digitally write this down and save it.)

_____

_____

_____

_____

_____

_____

_____

_____

_____

_____

CONCLUSION

It has been the most amazing experience thus far writing this book. It's difficult to put into words the growth that I have seen in myself over the years, and I hope that I was able to bring some of that to life. I feel a sense of fulfilment, as it has helped me to embrace the potentials within, while assisting others to build faith in themselves. You see, success is fleeting, but if it is founded on active principles backed by excellent assurance results. You can return to its longevity. I have poured out from my bank of knowledge, and I am confident you will never be the same again after reading this. At worst, you get a great laugh from my poor attempts at humor. What this book is to reach out to people with a drive and passion for success and bring their thoughts to fruition with workable and easy-to-take steps that promise results. Your experiences with this book will change the way you view success, and I am banking on your willingness to try new things. Don't hold back! Trust the process, and you will be the better for it.

We started out by talking about the role of passion in being successful and how passion is vital to your happiness. You should create a plan to be successful as you dream big and even more significantly.

These steps form the foundation on which our journey to success is built on, and, if you get these steps right, every other thing will just snowball. Loving what you do is key to being excellent, and an appreciative person will always get the best out of any situation. You have to note that success doesn't guarantee joy, and it can be quite opposite.

We also dwelt on the issue of removing fear and doubt from your mind. The concern is the most destabilizing factor that hinders progress, and as you define what success is to you, it becomes easier for you to get up and fight even after a challenging time. Learn the art of goal setting and don't be afraid to set goals so big that others call you crazy. Believing in yourself isn't negotiable. No one should play that role for you. As you build faith in yourself, it helps you pay more attention to detail, as you will tend to think before you act.

Surrounding yourself with other successful people will help stimulate your mind for success and ensure you stay motivated. You cannot afford to go back to the past. You should be all about the future, which is the reason communication is critical. Learning to communicate will keep you connected to the present reality. This book is a way to give back to others what so many have given to me. Once you experience success, help bring others along and mentor if you find it in your heart. Being an organized individual is key to staying on top. It keeps you alert and in a state of professional well-being. What is a success without good health? Your health is wealth. It should be the priority. Above all, you have to start early, start now, and start happy. Success is at your door, open up and milk it for what it's worth. After all, you were born to win!

DeJuan Gossett is a vice president/employee benefit consultant with USI Insurance Services. His passion for helping others drives him in this profession, as the mitigation of risk and cost is vital to not only the success of the companies that he represents but to their employees, as costs for healthcare continue to rise. He has 3 children ages 11, 7, and 3 years old. In his spare time, he is a volunteer football coach with the Union Raiders Football Club, and he serves on many boards in the Cincinnati area. DeJuan is the president of the board of directors for JC Baker & Associates/ Motivate 2 Gradu8 Inc., which carries the mission of ensuring that all students have an opportunity and the resources to graduate at each level of the education system. DeJuan is also vice chair of Corryville Catholic Elementary School, a member of the Cincinnati Scholarship Foundation board, a member of the United Way Herbert R Brown Steering Committee, and, most recently, has been appointed to the board of the Southwest Ohio Region Workforce Investment Board.

www.ingramcontent.com/pod-product-compliance
Lightning Source LLC
Chambersburg PA
CBHW071454070426
42452CB00039B/1351